Techniques of Writing
Business Letters,
Memos, and Reports

Techniques of Writing Business Letters, Memos, and Reports

Courtland L. Bovee

Roxbury Publishing Company

TECHNIQUES OF WRITING BUSINESS LETTERS, MEMOS, AND REPORTS (Second Edition)

Second edition 1989. Copyright • 1978 Courtland L. Bovee. All rights reserved under International and Pan-American Copyright Conventions. No part of this publication may be reproduced, stored in a retrieval system, or transmitted in any form or by any means, electronic, mechanical, photocopying, recording, or otherwise without prior written permission of the author and publisher.

Library of Congress Card Number 77-92913

ISBN 0-935732-15-2

Manufactured in the United States of America 10 9 8 7 6 5 4 3 2 1

The first edition of this book was published by Banner Books.

ROXBURY PUBLISHING COMPANY
P.O. Box 491044
Los Angeles, California 90049
(213) 653-1068

FORWARD TO THE SECOND EDITION

Most business people spend a good deal of time writing. Their aim is to promote sales, profits, and good will. But the results often are just the opposite. Far too many business messages are wordy, unclear, even antagonistic. The result is wasted time, needless expense, lost sales, and disgruntled customers.

This book shows you the way to effective business writing. You not only are told what to do—you are shown, step by step. Short, practical exercises enable you to practice what you learn. Areas which require more mastery can be pinpointed.

The author provides clear examples of good and ineffective use of language. He examines difficult writing problems and offers solid solutions. These techniques will aid both the time-pressed executive and the busy office worker. Men and women at all levels will find this book a valuable time-saving guide to improved written communication.

In this book, the author reveals the following secrets of successful writing:

- Action-getting phrases that sell ideas and motivate others to do what you want them to do.

- Three words that can destroy favorable reactions to what you write. (Avoid them for the important reasons explained on page 38.)

- How to turn negative words into positive words.

- A simple formula that makes your writing more readable.

- How to keep your friends and customers—even when you have to criticize, scold, or decline a request.

- Writing shortcuts that put across your ideas quickly and concisely.

- Writing tips that turn adversaries into friends. How to make written communication work for you instead of against you.

Effective business writing is determined not only by what you say, but by how you say it. *Techniques of Writing Business Letters, Memos, and Reports* shows you how to say it best.

TABLE OF CONTENTS

PART I.
PRINCIPLES OF WRITTEN COMMUNICATION

PART II.
PRINCIPLES OF WRITING LETTERS

LETTER WRITING TECHNIQUES

LETTER MECHANICS

PART III.
PRINCIPLES OF WRITING MEMORANDUMS

PART IV.
PRINCIPLES OF WRITING FORMAL REPORTS

PART V.
PRINCIPLES OF WRITING INFORMAL REPORTS

PART VI.
APPENDIXES

PART I.
PRINCIPLES OF WRITTEN COMMUNICATION

GENERAL TECHNIQUES

WRITE TO PEOPLE

Communication happens only when you write something that somebody else reads and understands. For this, you must use words and concepts that mean the same thing to you and to your reader.

In other words, you must adapt your writing to your reader.

Start with a clear mental idea of who your reader is. What is his work, his educational background? How does he think? What does he know about the subject? Now use his vocabulary, his way of thinking, when you write.

But, be careful that you don't slip and write down to him (he may get annoyed). And don't write over his head (he may not understand).

If there will be a group of readers, instead of just one, visualize the group. Find the near-lowest level of the group. Write to that level.

MAKE READING EASY

Too much writing is difficult to read. That is, the intended readers find it difficult to read. Magazines like *Reader's Digest* and *Time*, for example, are aimed at a different level of education and understanding than the highly technical professional and trade journals.

There are many methods for making writing easier to read. But sometimes it's well to know more about the communication problem before trying to apply any of the methods.

Probably the most popular of today's formulas for measuring readability is the Gunning Fog Index.

Fog Index

1. Count the number of words in a writing sample at least 100 words long. Count the number of sentences. Count independent clauses as if they were separate sentences. That is, if a period can be used to replace a comma, semicolon, or colon, count each clause as a sentence.

2. Determine the average number of words in each sentence.

3. Count the number of polysyllable words (three or more syllables each) in each hundred words. Don't count (1) capitalized words, unless they start a sentence; (2) combinations of short, easy words (businessman, nevertheless); (3) verb forms made into three-syllable words by the addition of "ed" or "es" (repeat-ed, address-es).

4. Add the average sentence length and the percentage of polysyllable words. Multiply by .4. This is the Fog Index. It corresponds roughly to the minimum school grade level at which the writing is easy to read.

Most business writing should score between 8 and 11.

STYLE IS A HELP

Good writing style is important to good communication, but the writing style should not be obvious. The reader wants to know what you have to say, not how you say it. An inappropriate style—too familiar, flippant, stiff, formal, or whatever—is distracting. It interferes with information flow.

The two main ways your writing style can intrude are:

(1) Use of the wrong writing level for the situation.

(2) Violation of some of the more common conventions of word choice, spelling, punctuation, grammar, and sentence structure.

Avoid these, and help your writing.

CORRECTING FAULTS IN TECHNIQUE

WORDS

The foundation of all good writing is the selection of words that describe or explain. There are general techniques for this, as has already been pointed out. But there are also specific techniques—word selection methods that can be used in most situations.

Strong Words. Stick with nouns and verbs as much as you can; they're the action words. Don't rely on adjectives and adverbs to tell your story; they call for subjective judgments, and business communication should be objective.

Weak	*Strong*
wealthy businessman	tycoon
business prosperity	boom
fall	plummet

Familiar Words. You will communicate best if you mostly use words that are familiar to your reader—specifically, however, familiar within his personal frames of reference. Words that are familiar to one reader, or group of readers, could be meaningless, or almost so, to another.

Cliches (see *Obsolete Language*) are an exception to this use of the familiar. Words and phrases that we have heard too often tend to turn off our minds at least a little.

We tend to slide across them to whatever is coming up next, and communication effectiveness drops.

Unfamiliar	*Familiar*
ascertain	find out, learn
consummate	close, bring about
peruse	read, study

Short Words. Make an effort to use short words. They tend to communicate better than long words. This is why the Fog Index includes polysyllable words as a difficulty factor.

Long

During the preceding year, the company was able to accelerate productive operations.

The action was predicated on the assumption that the company was operating at a financial deficit.

The president acceded to the proposition to nullify the contractual relationship.

Short

Last year the company was able to speed up operations.

The action was based on the belief that the company was losing money.

The president agreed to break the contract.

Concrete Words. The dividing line between abstract and concrete words is hard to define, since all words have something of the abstract about them. In general, abstract words usually have a greater number of meanings, most of them somewhat vague, and your reader has to try to interpret which meanings apply. Concrete words are those that give your reader something he can mentally picture, because they tie closely to the reader's experience.

Abstract	*Concrete*
sizable loss	34 percent loss
near future	on Wednesday
worksaving machine	performs the work of five men

Active Words. Verbs are the strongest words, and they are at their strongest when they are active, rather than passive, verbs. Active-voice verbs show their subjects in action; passive-voice verbs act on their subjects. While the passive is needed for variety, and has definite uses (as in rule books), the active voice strengthens and shortens sentences.

Passive

A sales increase of 32 percent occurred last month.

The new procedure is thought to be superior by the president.

The office will be cleaned by the janitor.

Active

Sales increased 32 percent last month.

The president thinks the new procedure is superior.

The janitor will clean the office.

Camouflaged Words. Watch for these endings in the words you use (check the polysyllable words): -ion, -tion, -ing, -ment, -ant, -ent, -ence, -ancy, -ency. Most of these endings are used to change verbs into nouns and adjectives. In effect, they are camouflaged verbs. Get rid of them and strengthen your writing.

Poor

Implementation of the rules was effected by the manager.

Adaptation to the new office environment was made easily by the personnel.

Verification of the shipments is made weekly.

Improved

The manager implemented the rules.

The personnel adapted easily to the new office environment.

Shipments are verified weekly.

Technical Words. Use them with caution. You've been advised to use familiar words—words that are familiar within your reader's frames of reference. For most business writing, this means you should assume your reader is a layman, with limited technical knowledge of the subject. Even where your reader does have extensive technical knowledge, too many technical terms increase the Fog Index number, and make your writing hard to understand.

Unnecessary Words. Most business writing could do with a pruning job. To reduce unnecessary words, start with a clear idea of what you want to say. After writing, go over your writing with a pencil and cut out every word that is not essential to your meaning.

Poor	*Improved*
consensus of opinion	consensus
first and foremost	(either word, but not both)
just recently	recently
true facts	facts
anxious and eager	(either word, but not both)
ask the question	ask
basic fundamentals	fundamentals
exactly identical	identical

PHRASES

Replaceable Phrases. There are many compound phrases that don't compound the meaning. They are either repetitious or have one-word equivalents. Frequently, "legalistic" language is an offender: "This is to inform you that we have" (we have); "for the sum of" (for); "in the event that" (if); "on the occasion of" (on); "prior to the start of" (before). Redundancy is a somewhat lesser flaw: "Visible to the eye" (visible); "surrounded on all sides" (surrounded). Relative pronouns—"who," "that," "which"—frequently cause clutter. Sometimes, even articles are excessive (mostly too many "the's").

Poor	*Improved*
a small number of	few
during the time that	while
due to the fact that	because
in the same way	similarly
at an early date	soon
remember the fact that	remember
not in a position	unable
most of the time	usually
in view of the fact that	since
until such time	when
we are of the opinion that	we believe
with reference to	about
without further delay	now (immediately)
as a result of	because
for the month of December	for December
typewriters which are of the portable type	portable typewriters

Infinitive Substitutes. Whenever a phrase substitutes for an infinitive, the sentence will be longer, and some of your meaning will be vague.

Poor

In order to be a successful writer, hard work is necessary.

He went to the library for the purpose of studying.

The employer increased the salaries so that he could improve morale.

Improved

To be a successful writer, hard work is necessary.

He went to the library to study.

The employer increased salaries to improve morale.

Obsolete Phrases. Obsolete phrases are simply out-of-date phrases. They contribute to tiresome sentences. They increase sentence length. They come between you and your reader. Perhaps the best way to eliminate them is to ask yourself: "Would I say it this way if I were talking to this man face to face?"

Obsolete	*Up to Date*
beg to state	(omit)
as per your letter	as in your letter (do not mix Latin and English)

Obsolete	Up to Date
hoping to hear from you soon, we remain	(omit)
in response to same	in response to it
yours of the 12th	your letter of June 12
awaiting your reply, we are	(omit)
in due course	today; tomorrow (or a specific time or date)
permit me to say that	(permission is not necessary; just say what you wish)
we are in receipt of	we have received
pursuant to	(omit)
in closing, I'd like to say	(omit)
according to our records	we find
attached herewith is	here is
kindly advise	please let us know
this will acknowledge	thank you for
contents duly noted	followed in every detail
as stated above	as I have said
under separate cover	in another envelope; by parcel post

SENTENCES

Short Sentences. Long sentences are usually harder to understand than short sentences. Most business writing should have an average sentence length of not over 20 words. This is the average, not a ceiling. Your writing should contain both long and short sentences to keep it interesting. But short sentences are easier to understand; they are not too jam-packed with information that must all be absorbed at once. Most long sentences can be readily broken up into two or more shorter sentences. Practicing the word selection methods will help you start thinking in terms of short sentences.

Poor

This memorandum is being distributed with the blueprints which show the final version of the new offices at our new Los Angeles headquarters and are to be used later for discussion at the next board meeting which is to be held on August 1.

Improved

This memorandum is being distributed with the blueprints. These blueprints show the final version of the Los Angeles headquarter offices. Later they will be used at the August 1 board meeting.

Pompous Sentences. "Pompous" is a word that is gradually fading from use. But pompous language is still with us. It shows as puffed-up, roundabout sentences, with a high percentage of big (polysyllable) words. Gobbledygook is a good example of it. When we think of gobbledygook we think of governmentese. However, the flaw is not confined to bureaucrats. Many business writers use a phrase or a whole clause when a well-chosen verb would convey far more meaning. So, don't stiffen up, use big words or trite expressions, or get involved in complicated and formal sentences. Write to express, not impress.

Poor

Upon procurement of additional supplies, I will initiate fulfillment of your order.

Perusal of the records indicate a substantial deficit for the preceding accounting period due to the utilization of antiquated mechanisms.

Because of the inauguration of the merger, there has been a diminution in the hiring of office workers.

Improved

I will fill your order when I receive more supplies.

The records show a company loss last year because old equipment was used.

There has been a decrease in hiring office workers because of the merger.

Overloaded Sentences. Overloaded sentences contain a lot of unnecessary words. This frequently shows up as a series of sentences that start with the same word or words, and the repetition soon grows deadly. But repetition often shows up within sentences (constant references to "the contract", for example). And sometimes the repetition is of a concept, rather than the word itself (modern up-to-date equipment; modern equipment). Use of passive verbs will give you too many words (can be observed to be decreasing vs. decreases). And there are words and phrases that add nothing to the meaning of the sentence in many instances (which are, in addition to).

Poor

In my opinion, I think the decision was right.

During the time he was a traveling salesman, Mr. Jones was earning $25,000.

Management is involved in the task of reviewing each contract.

Improved

I think the decision was right.

While he was a traveling salesman, Mr. Jones was earning $25,000.

Management is reviewing each contract.

Undue Enthusiasm. An occasional intensifier lends emphasis. But too many ruin your writing.

Poor

We are extremely pleased to offer you a position on our staff of exceptionally skilled and highly educated employees. The work offers extraordinary challenges and a very large salary.

Improved

We are pleased to offer you a position on our staff of skilled and educated employees. The work offers challenges and a large salary.

Crowded-Together Sentences. These happen when you write a series of related sentences, but keep connecting them with each other by "and" instead of ending each with a period. You can improve your sentences by using only one subject.

Poor

The magazine will be published January 1, and I'd better meet the deadline if I want my article included.

Improved

The magazine will be published January 1. I'd better meet the deadline if I want my article included.

Hedging Sentences. Sometimes you have to write "it seems that," or "there appears to be" in order to avoid stating a judgment as a fact. But when you have too many hedges, particularly several in a sentence, you aren't really saying anything.

Poor

I believe that Mr. Johnson's employment record seems to show that he appears capable of handling the position.

Improved

Mr. Johnson's employment record shows that he is capable of handling the position.

Pronoun Starters. If you start a sentence with "it" or "there", odds are the sentence could be shorter. (It would be appreciated vs. Please.)

Poor

It would be appreciated if you would sign the lease today.

There are five employees in this division who were late to work today.

Improved

Please sign the lease today.

Five employees in this division were late to work today.

Parallelism. When you have two or more similar (parallel) ideas to present, either in one sentence or in several, it is a good idea to present each idea in the same pattern. If you don't, the lack of parallelism will create an awkward style.

Poor

When Miss Simms arrived, she had been drenched with rain, bombarded with telephone calls, and her boss shouted at her.

Mr. Reynolds dictated the letter and next he signed it, and left the office.

Improved

When Miss Simms arrived, she had been drenched with rain, bombarded with telephone calls, and shouted at by her boss.

Mr. Reynolds dictated the letter, signed it, and left the office.

Awkward Pointers. To save words, business writers point readers' attention backward with expressions like these: as mentioned above; the above mentioned; the aforementioned; the former; the latter; respectively. These words cause the reader to go back to the beginning of the sentence to get the meaning of the message, a process which hinders effective communication.

Poor

Typewriter ribbons for legal secretaries and beginning clerks are distributed by the Law Office and Stenographic Office respectively.

Improved

Typewriter ribbons for legal secretaries are distributed by the Law Office; those for beginning clerks, by the Stenographic Office.

Misassembled Sentences. These are more commonly known as "dangling modifiers," which doesn't tell anybody much. A misassembled sentence is one where you have something in the wrong place. When you have a modifier or clause in the wrong place in the sentence, you wind up with something that is not to be taken seriously at best, and is grotesque at worst.

Poor

Walking to the office, a red sports car passed him.

Going down in the elevator, the office was in a different world.

Working as fast as possible, the budget soon was ready.

Improved

A red sports car passed him while he was walking to the office.

The office seemed to be in a different world as he rode down in the elevator.

The committee, working as fast as possible, soon had the budget ready.

PARAGRAPHS

Paragraph Unity. Each paragraph should contain one overall topic or idea. When you mix things together, communication sometimes gets mixed up.

Topic Sentences. The simplest way to establish paragraph unity is to use topic sentences—preferably as the first sentence of each paragraph. In such writing, your reader could read the first sentence of each paragraph and know your basic story. He could read all of each paragraph and know the details of your story. While topic sentences can be placed elsewhere in paragraphs, this requires considerable writing skill.

A majority of the researchers think the public will buy the product. Of the seven researchers interviewed, four think the product will gain immediate acceptance, two believe that some development of the market will have to take place, and one feels that this is a poor time for market entry. All of the researchers were unanimous in their belief that product performance was excellent in test marketing.

Short Paragraphs. You've had the experience of opening a magazine or book and finding solid pages of type—and, on other occasions, of finding many pages with short paragraphs and all that white space between them. If you're like the average reader, you tackled the first with reluctance, the second willingly. ■

PART II.
PRINCIPLES OF
WRITING LETTERS

LETTER WRITING TECHNIQUES

ORGANIZATION STEPS

If you don't plan the letter first, instead of trying to think it out as you write, you can't effectively write anything more than a very simple letter. Try asking yourself these five questions:

1. Who is the reader? (See *Write to People,* at the start of this book.)

2. What do I want the letter to accomplish?

3. What type of letter am I writing? (See *Types of Letters,* next page.)

4. What information and ideas will accomplish what I want here?

5. Considering the type of letter I'm writing, what is the best sequence for the information and the ideas?

TYPES OF LETTERS

Neutral. Put your topics into groups. Varied choices for the structure of the letter (these may be reversed) include: (1) general to specific, (2) cause to effect, (3) order of importance, (4) nearest to farthest (space relations), or (5) order of happening (time relations).

Good News. Put the good news (main idea) in the first sentence. Then follow with any necessary details in their order of importance or natural sequence. Consider ending the letter by recalling the benefits of the good news.

Bad News. The basic point to keep in mind for this type of letter is that bluntness is bad. Start off the first paragraph with statements of agreement (a "buffer"). The buffer should be relevant to the situation as well as being pleasant (perhaps agreeing with something the reader has said). Avoid, in the *first* paragraph, implying the letter contains bad news or that you're saying yes or no.

Poor (without buffer)

We regret to inform you that it is against company policy to supply anyone outside the company with collection letter samples.

Improved (with a buffer)

You are certainly right about the need for a business student to have a thorough understanding of collection letter psychology.

In the second paragraph, work your way through the problem (always giving reasons before a direct or implied refusal). Find an area of favorable interest, agreement, or reassurance to use as an ending of the letter.

Persuasive. Get the reader's attention quickly by promising or offering him a benefit you are sure will interest him. Give evidence (the kind he will find believable) backing up the benefit. Then ask him—with confidence—to do what it is you want him to do.

PERSUASION

Tone. The whole tone of a letter should suggest that you are interested in the reader's problems, and in helping him solve them. Only oral communication—in person or by telephone—has more immediacy and persuasion power than a letter. And you have a captive audience who will be retaining a permanent record of your statements. Tone is critical to your letters: how it sounds to the reader; the overall impression it conveys to, and leaves imprinted on, his mind. Good tone is ruined by using harsh words or phrases.

Poor	*Improved*
you failed to enclose	you did not enclose
the alleged loss	the loss you refer to
you claim that	we understand that
we hereby deny your claim	we cannot honor your claim
you neglected to send	you did not send
it is our definite policy	it is our practice
in which you assert	you tell us

Poor	Improved
if we were at fault	please accept our apologies
we request that you send us	please send us
it is not our policy to	we do not

"You" Viewpoint. Too many letters have an "I" or "we" viewpoint, which causes the writer to sound selfish and not interested in the reader. The message tells what the writer wants; the reader is expected to go along with it. If you want to get your point of view across, convey information, or persuade the reader, you've got to talk in terms of his interests, hopes, wishes, and preferences. Talk about the reader, and you are talking about the most interesting thing in the world—him. Good writing psychology requires that you present your message in the light of the reader's thinking rather than your own.

"I" or "We"

To help us process this order, we must ask for another copy of the requisition.

We are pleased to announce our new flight schedule from San Diego to Los Angeles which is any hour on the hour.

We offer the typewriter ribbons in three colors: black, blue, and green.

"You"

So that your order can be filled promptly, will you please send another copy of the requisition.

Now you can take a plane from San Diego to Los Angeles any hour on the hour.

Take your pick of the typewriter ribbons in three colors: black, blue, and green.

Positive vs. Negative Viewpoints. Most people will respond more favorably to a positive viewpoint than to a negative. Yet, surprisingly, much business writing is about the darker side of the picture. Use these methods in your writing:

1. Make sure you stress what things are or what they will be, instead of what they aren't or won't be. Stress what you can do, what you will do—not what you haven't done, can't do, or won't do.

2. Don't use words with negative connotations if you can avoid them.

Poor

We cannot conduct a seminar with less than 20 participants.

You will never be sorry that you own this business writing book.

We are sorry that we cannot send you the books until after August 1.

Improved

We always conduct a seminar with 20 participants or more.

You will always be grateful that you own this business writing book.

We can promise you delivery of the books after August 1.

Euphemisms. To euphemize is to substitute an inoffensive, mild word for a word which may be offensive, harsh, or blunt. When a writer euphemizes, he "puts a good face" on something. Calling a used car a "resale car" doesn't change its appearance or function, but it may soften the mental impression for people.

Possibly Offensive	*Inoffensive*
toilet paper	bathroom tissue
liquor store	package store
sweaty armpits	underarm wetness
constipated	irregular
high calorie food	high energy food

Confidence and Conviction. This is another aspect of negative viewpoints. Your writing should be straightforward and reasonable, so that the reader will have no doubts. Three words—if, hope, and trust—are the greatest destroyers of confidence and conviction. Be fully convinced in your own mind that your explanation is adequate, your suggestion legitimate and valuable to the reader, your decision the result of adequate evidence and logical, businesslike reasoning. You are then likely to write a positive letter, aimed squarely at the points to be made. You have a good chance to avoid equivocations, alternates, and maybe-this-maybe-that viewpoints.

Poor

We hope this recommendation you requested will be helpful.

If you'd like to order, mail us the reply card.

We trust you'll extend your service contract.

Improved

We're glad to make this recommendation you requested.

To order, mail the reply card.

By extending your service contract, you can continue to enjoy topnotch performance from your equipment.

Warmth. You can make all sorts of mistakes in your letters, yet still leave your readers with a good feeling, if the letters have the magic intangible of personal warmth. Somehow, warmth is more difficult in writing than it is in speaking, in face-to-face relations. Essentially, warmth is an aspect—possibly even the measure—of the "you" viewpoint. You show not only concern for the reader's problems, but interest in his attitudes, and possibly even appreciation of the ways in which the situation is going to be helpful to you, too.

Parallel Experience. One way of touching the right spots inside your reader is to find a parallel situation in your own experience. Build your letter around this experience, or use what you learned as a basis for your letter.

Good Manners. Bad manners in writing take a wide variety of forms from the boy-did-I-tell-him-off nasty note, to the late reply, to not replying at all. If there's going to be a delay, let your correspondent know. And usually, anything more than a few days is a delay. The nasty notes and lack of replies are obvious examples of bad company manners.

LETTER MECHANICS

IMAGE

Company Image. Your company's image is the total impression a person has of the company. It includes what he sees, what he hears, and what he experiences about your company. Every business letter you write is therefore important (remember, only oral communication has more immediacy and persuasive power). Each of them is a part of the company image. Quality of letterhead and typing, copy position on the page, format, kind of typewriter face used, color of typewriter ribbon —all of these play a part in creating an impression of you and your company in the mind of the person you are writing to.

Letterheads. Be sure the letterhead reinforces the image you are trying to create. Lettering size, type, and colors should be carefully selected, as should the paper. The telephone number should be included. If the letterhead contains addresses of various company offices, be sure the reader can readily tell to which office he should send his reply.

Format. Technically, any format that is consistent is "correct." But extremes in format tend to distract, as do outmoded or not-immediately-clear formats. Keep the format as simple as possible, keep it consistent, keep it in the mainstream of current usage.

FORM LETTERS

Form letters are a quick way of handling routine replies. They can be "personalized" by developing a set of form paragraphs, then using the paragraphs to suit the situation. You might possibly even want to slightly modify some of the form paragraphs for individual replies. Short form letters can readily be worked out on the basis of everyday experience. But longer letters, particularly those made up of form paragraphs, require a research and development period. To do this:

1. Make a copy of every letter written for a four-week period.

2. Categorize the copies by major topics and sub-topics.

3. Select the frequently written letters that can be converted to form letters. Do the same for individual paragraphs.

4. Standardize the letters and paragraphs.

5. Make readjustments every 12 months.

PART III.
PRINCIPLES OF WRITING MEMORANDUMS

PURPOSES

The memo or memo report is a cross between the full-fledged report and an intracompany letter. It is a major factor in intracompany communications. Because of its importance, it should not be written hastily ("I'll just send out a bulletin"). It should be written with all the care you would give a letter to a customer, and should use all applicable techniques of letter and report writing. When you write a memorandum, you are out to accomplish one or more of the following:

1.   To provide exactly the same information to a number of people.

2.   To establish a record of discussions at a conference or meeting.

3.   To establish a record of decisions or agreements.

4.   To transmit information, policies, or directives to an individual or individuals.

FORMAT

If you use a printed form, preferably include company name or logo, and an overall heading such as Memorandum, Memo, or the like. Print "To", "From," and "Subject" flush left, and double-spaced; use a colon after each of these items. If you do not use a printed form, follow this basic pattern, but consider the inclusion of "Copy To" as applicable. With printed forms, "cc:" is usually put at the bottom of the page, with the names or initials following. When filling in the information for the top-left headings, align the first letters of the entries. The date ordinarily goes in the upper-right corner.

If all readers will recognize all individuals on the routing, you may use initials (including your own). If not, use last names and initials, or full names, depending on the people involved.

Try to avoid a set of straight paragraphs, one after the other. Break things up with headings, itemizations, tables, charts, so that the memorandum can be skimmed quickly both before and after reading. Single space between lines, double space between paragraphs.

COVERAGE

Organization of a memorandum is similar to that of a letter (see *Letter Writing Techniques*). If you are making a recommendation, verify your information and information sources. Include alternatives to your recommendation only where they have positive value (omit "on the other hand" alternatives). Be sure you have touched all bases, including those in your logic. Include effective dates, time frames, places, names of people concerned.

STYLE

Limit yourself to the stated subject; and the identification of the subject should be specific, not general. Cover only "must know" information and concepts. Avoid "should know" items, and shun "nice to know" items. (Incidentally, this approach is very good for all writing.) Follow the writing techniques in Parts I and II of this manual. Make special efforts to use short words and short sentences.

TONE

Keep in mind that copies of the memo usually are going to more than one person, even though primarily addressed to one person. Avoid sharp imperatives and accusations. Stay objective, but stay human. ■

PART IV.
PRINCIPLES OF WRITING FORMAL REPORTS

TYPES OF REPORTS

Introduction. Reports may be grouped into three overall types: informational, examinational, and analytical, as described below. However, each of these may, in turn, be in one of two categories: (1) day-to-day operational reports; (2) reports having to do with organizational change. Reports in the first category will ordinarily be shorter, and less complex.

Informational. These simply present information, as in an annual P&L statement. No attempt is made to interpret or evaluate the information.

Examinational. These present and interpret information. They do not present solutions to problems.

Analytical. These present and interpret information, draw conclusions, and make recommendations.

REPORT PLANNING

Problem Determination. The problem (the reason for the report's existence) may be simple, complex, and/or vaguely defined. Additional research may be necessary—others within the company, outside experts, library material, etc.—before the problem becomes clear-cut enough that you can write it down with assurance. You may also want to get a consensus on the written problem before going any further.

Problem Factors. These may be of three types: (1) subtopics of the main topic; (2) hypotheses for research and review; (3) bases to use for comparisons.

DATA RESEARCH

Research Methods. You may use one or more of the following methods:

1. Company records. Check in-house data-production, sales, marketing, accounting, inspection, shipping, etc.

2. Experiment or test. This is frequently used in marketing, as when a new approach is used in a small market to test the approach before making a major investment in a new campaign.

3. Observation. Here you simply watch. You observe the situation as it actually exists.

4. Consulting/Questioning. You can go to outside experts as competent information sources: consultants, associations, other businessmen, etc. Or

you can set up a questionnaire, formal or informal, and record answers to a planned pattern of questions.

5. Publications. These may be in your company library, or in a number of outside libraries: public, university, association, municipal, federal, etc. And certain basic sources—encyclopedias, trade directories, biographical directories, various federal government census and survey publications, books on information sources, indexes—can serve as starting points for research directions.

Note-Taking. No matter what research methods you use, don't rely on your memory. This means note-taking, perhaps supplemented by photography and tape-recording. Good note-taking requires an orderly plan to start with. You need criteria (the plan) to determine what to get on tape or word-for-word on paper, and what you can paraphrase, note down in detail, or summarize. Notes should preferably be put on file cards, if the information to be gathered is extensive. This lets you readily set up new sub-topics as they appear. It also lets you rearrange information into new sequences to suit new data or new data groupings.

DATA ORGANIZATION

Data Grouping. If data is not already arranged by subjects at the end of note-taking, groupings of data must be established—sub-topics, categories for tabulations, separate tests performed, etc. During this process, check the data for completeness, consistency, seeming errors, etc.

Outline Requirements. The initial grouping of data does not necessarily establish an outline for the report. In outlining, your purpose is to arrange the data in their clearest and most meaningful form. The outline will also establish the table of contents (if the report is long enough to warrant one), and the headings to be used within the text.

The conventional sequence of elements in the long report is from introduction through data to summary (informational reports), conclusions (examinational reports), or recommendations (analytical reports). You can also start with the summary, conclusions, or recommendations, following that with the supporting data.

In either event, the main body of the data is best arranged in branch-chain fashion. Here, you start with the main topic (subject), and divide that into a minimum number of sub-topics (preferably two) that are equal to each other and are immediately subordinate to the main topic. This same procedure is followed in descending levels of subordination until the lowest level is reached. Headings can then be established for each outline element at each level. The outline then can be made formal (Arabic, Roman, and alphabetical symbols) or informal (headings and sub-headings).

Another possible arrangement for the main body of data is by categories. Division into categories could be by time periods, place, quantity, order of importance of subject matter, etc.

Headings in the outline may be of two types: topic, which simply identify the immediate data grouping; or subjective, which summarize or provide a brief commentary on the data grouping. Both may be used within the same outline, but parallelism of construction is important. That is, in any particular sequence of equal level headings, all should be of one type or the other, rather than a mixture of the two.

REPORT ELEMENTS

The basic areas of a formal report are: front matter, introductory material, report body, summary/conclusions/recommendations, and appended matter. There may also be "enclosures," appended matter submitted as separate reference or supplementing documents. These areas are made up of the elements described in the following paragraphs. A very formal and lengthy report could contain all of these elements; ordinarily, only certain ones turn out to be essential.

Title Fly. Not often used. It contains only the title of the report-although this is sometimes supported by artwork intended to establish the tone of the report.

Title Page. The title page contains all necessary identifying information—report title, number, writer, company, department, address, date, etc., as applicable.

Letter of Authorization. Used only where a written authorization was required for the report. Preferably, authorization should be described briefly in the preface, if required to be mentioned at all.

Letter of Transmittal. This letter basically states, "here is the report." It may further contain statements as to follow-up action by the writer, action requested of the reader, etc. Location of the letter (and inclusion of it) varies. In a report with a title fly page, any letter should probably be separate from the report. In many instances, the letter is the first page of the report. The Letter of Transmittal and Synopsis are sometimes combined, particularly in short reports.

Table of Contents. A table of contents is a useful guide in all but extremely short reports. If there is a number of tables, charts, and illustrations, give each group its own listing.

Synopsis. The synopsis has many names: summary, abstract, epitome, precis, etc. Frequently, it is a simple abstract, containing the essential data items of the report. It then usually appears at the top of the first page of the introductory material. Where the report does not contain a synopsis, the preface provides a brief initial summary of the report, largely intended for those readers not likely to read the entire report.

Introduction. The introduction can cover a large number of elements: authorization information, report origin, purpose of the report, scope (parameters), data sources, data collection and analysis information, historical background, definitions, description of the report's structure, etc.

Report Body. See *Outline Requirements.*
Summary/Conclusions/Recommendations. See *Outline Requirements.*

Appendixes. The report body should contain only material directly applicable to the report. Supplementary information belongs in appendixes, with each appendix covering only one main topic.

Bibliography. Used primarily when the content of the report is largely a result of bibliographical research.

Index. Used only in lengthy reports. If there is good usage of major and minor headings in the report, the index can be made up of only the headings, and all topics and sub-topics will then be mentioned.

DATA INTERPRETATION

Facts alone do not solve problems. Data in the report therefore must be presented in logical groupings and arrangements.

The Data Base. The data on which interpretations are based must be unquestionably reliable. It must be representative of elements of the problem; that is, there must be a one-to-one relation between problem phases and the data groupings on which interpretations are based. Every conclusion must be supported by adequate data—conclusions not directly supported by data don't belong in the report.

Logic. The reasons for the groupings of data should be easily grasped, and should be logical. When comparing groups of data to arrive at interpretations, the groups themselves must be comparable to start with. Similarly, cause-and-effect relationships must be truly in that sequence; no valid conclusions can be drawn from data groups that are merely associated. When analyzing a set of factors, be sure they're all there; missing factors will cause incorrect or misleading conclusions. If you are using mathematical tools—such as averages, medians, modes, ratios—stay fully aware of both the uses and limitations of each. Their usage must be logical for conclusions to be meaningful.

Evaluation Attitudes. Important in data interpretation is complete objectivity. Examine the pros and cons of each situation with an open mind, taking a look at both sides of the matter for objective comparison. While avoiding deliberate bias, be on the lookout for any unconscious biases you may have. When conclusions are formed, avoid the kind of enthusiasm that leads to exaggeration of their importance. And don't try to put an interpretation on every aspect of the problem. Sometimes you won't be able to work out any. Sometimes you may wind up with several interpretations, or with one that must be stated with qualifications.

Checking. Talk over your problems, appraisals, and interpretations with others who are knowledgeable. If possible, check interpretations by testing them. If not possible, find what seems reasonable on the basis of your own experience, or the experience of someone more knowledgeable than you.

Interpretation Procedures. The first step is to relate adequate data to individual phases of the problem. Next, make every interpretation that has merit, even though this may give you multiple interpretations for some bit or grouping of data. Review the interpretations in their entirety, as a set. Select those that have the most merit. Drop the others; if any of these are retained, develop qualifying explanations. Develop conclusions from the interpretations that prove to have merit. Develop recommendations from the conclusions. Through all of this, stay aware that your reader's mind is going to have to be guided from the data through the developing patterns of interpretations. You must provide a reasonable (and preferably easy) path for him to follow.

COMMUNICATION ESSENTIALS

Believability. Be objective and logical in your writing attitude and style. This is the surest way to achieve believability in the report. You may also find impersonal (third person) writing will help the believability of your writing, particularly in a major formal report. In shorter, informal reports, personal (I's, we's, or you's) writing may create a rapport with the reader, without disturbing either objectivity or believability.

Viewpoint. Consistency in time-viewpoint will reduce illogical shifts from one tense to another. The viewpoint can be either that of looking back to a past time or reporting in a present time.

Coherence. When each fact is in its logical place, and the inter-relationships between facts and between facts and report plan are clear to the reader, the report may be said to have overall coherence. Some devices for this: transitional words and sentences between lesser parts of the report; introductory and preview paragraphs for major relationships; concluding and summary paragraphs to mark stages of progress.

Style. The text of the report should be interesting and it can be so if you follow the general techniques given in Part I. Especially important to reports is that reader reaction is to "interesting facts," rather than "beautiful writing".

Excerpts. Data from other documents may be paraphrased (put in your own words) or may be used verbatim (exactly the same as the original). Paraphrased material ordinarily need not be specially sorted out from the remainder of your text, but verbatim material should be. If the verbatim passage is four lines or less, run it right in with your own writing, setting it off with quotation marks. If five lines or more, set it in from both right and left margins of the body text, as a separate block. Quotation marks are not needed for this. If you are omitting parts of the original passage, use an ellipsis (...) at the point of omission.

Footnotes. Inform the reader of the sources of paraphrased and quoted material either by direct reference in the text or by footnotes. Failure to footnote such material is to commit plagiarism—with a consequent reduction in the believability of your report. Footnotes are usually placed at the bottom of the page, but may be grouped and placed at the end of the report, possibly as identifying numbers within the bibliography. In either event, a superscript number is typed half a line higher than the text line, at the end of the quoted material. The numbers may be consecutive on the page, or within each section or chapter, or within the entire report.

Bibliography. A bibliography may list only those documents used as source material in developing portions of the report, or it may be a more extensive listing that includes published material germane to the subject. In the former instance, the sequence may be that of the footnote numbers used in the text, although alphabetical listing is preferable. List the author with his last name first (keep co-author's names in normal sequence). Use hanging indentation form: first line of an entry flush left, remaining lines indented.

ILLUSTRATIONS AND TABLES

Plan. Illustrations frequently are essential to business reports. Even when not essential, their use often improves communication. Illustrations may be used simply to supplement text, or they may be so closely related to the text that it would lose a good part of its meaning without them. The first method is the conventional method, especially for major and detailed studies. The second method is more likely to be used in reports that are intended to be read quickly and easily. Many reports use both methods, as appropriate.

Location. Illustrations and tables may be placed at the back of the report, or may be included within the main body of the report. The first method may prove convenient if they primarily supplement the text, or if some of them are bulky (foldouts). Preferably, illustrations and tables should be placed within the body of the report, and as close as possible to the related text. Location here will then depend in part on the type of illustration, and in part on the method of reproduction. If the report is to be duplicated in only a few copies, it may be necessary to place illustrations (particularly photographic ones) on individual pages, no matter what their size. If the report is to be printed, efforts should be made to include them on the same pages with text, since this adds interest to the reading process.

General Mechanics. Illustrations should be sized appropriate to their information content; that is, one with little information should be smaller than one with a great deal of information. Keep full-page illustrations within the page image area (the area within the page margins). Consider using a border around each illustration that is less than full-page. Provide captions and sequence numbers for each illustration and table. Numbers for illustrations and for tables are usually in separate sequences. Captions should be complete enough to relate easily to the applicable text. Place illustration captions at the bottom, table titles at the top. Footnotes and source acknowledgments are usually placed at the bottom, either under the illustration caption or at the bottom of the table (marked with the conventional footnote asterisk).

Tables. Tables should be constructed in whatever manner is conventional for the type of data being presented. This improves communication with your reader, since you are presenting the data in his terms. Symbology, abbreviations, footnotes, whether or not the tables are lined between columns-matters such as these should be adapted to the reader's own experience with similar data.

FINAL FORMAT

Physical Presentation. The physical appearance of your report should give a favorable first impression. However, the report should not be too elaborate, or the favorable first impression will fade. Covers should be suitable to the circumstances and the size of the report. A lengthy major report should perhaps have a durable hard cover. A short report could be put into a notebook binder, or stapled into a folder. In between are all sorts of hard and soft covers. Preferably, use a cover that will enable the report pages to lie flat while being read. Use a good quality paper for the original report. Standard 8 ½ x 11 paper should be used whenever possible; 8 ½ x 13 should be reserved for reports that contain long tables. Page layout, basically, is whatever looks good for the material being presented. In general, use margins of 1 ¼ " to 1 ½ " at top and sides, about half again as much at bottom.

Typing. The most readable typed page is single-spaced between lines, double-spaced between paragraphs, triple-spaced above centered headings. Here is a widely used heading schedule:

CENTERED HEADINGS

FIRST ORDER SIDE HEADINGS

Text below, either indented, or set flush left to form a block of copy.

Second Order Side Headings

Text same as above.

Third Order Side Headings. Text run in on the same line as the heading.

If further breakdowns are needed, use numbers, lower case letters, or bullets. (These should be avoided during the writing process, however, because they tend to break your thoughts into small fragments, thereby making the inter-relationships less obvious.)

Typing should be neat, typed with a good ribbon. If a selection of typewriters is available to you, pick one with a type that looks businesslike. Avoid typewriter faces that are quite large, quite small, or too "fancy" (such as italicized).

Marginals on the typed pages may include, in addition to the page number, chapter number, chapter name, or subject matter. Pages may be numbered within chapters, or in one sequence throughout the report. While page numbers are frequently put in the upper-right corner of the page, it is now more conventional to center them at the bottom of the page.

Special Formats. Special formats are required for the front matter and appended matter: title fly, title page, letters of authorization and transmittal, acknowledgments, table of contents, list of illustrations, list of tables, bibliography, index. The letters should appear as letters in whatever format is customary in your business. Report practices for the other pages are quite similar to the practices used in conventional business and technical text books. You can find examples in your own office. ■

PART V.
PRINCIPLES OF WRITING INFORMAL REPORTS

SCOPE

Informal reports are more common than formal reports. They are also much shorter, sometimes little more than a lengthy memorandum. However, their preparation is usually given more care than a memorandum, since they are junior-sized versions of formal reports. The "Report Elements" listed in Part IV are used as applicable. Illustrations and tables may be required.

TECHNIQUES

Plan the report, and research the data, just as you would for a formal report. The data organization is likely to be simpler, and note-taking need not be as extensive (perhaps not even on file cards). Arrangement of the main body of data is more likely to be by categories, since the branch-chain method may establish too detailed a breakdown for the size and type of report.

Introductory material can be frequently reduced to a brief introduction. Since the main purpose of the report is usually to handle an immediate or a day-to-day problem, the point of the report (summary/conclusions/recommendation) is immediately given, and is stated in more detail than in a formal report. The body of the report then follows.

Writing style is more frequently personal, rather than impersonal. The heading schedule will not have as many levels as the formal report, but will be more like the headings in memorandums. Coherence techniques (transitions, introductions, summaries) are needed less because the pattern of the report is simpler, and can be held in the mind merely by reference to the table of contents. ■

PART VI.
APPENDIXES

A. REFERENCES FOR BUSINESS WRITERS

For further information about written communication in business, you should consult the following directories:

ARTICLES: *Business Periodicals Index* and *Reader's Guide to Periodical Literature*

PERIODICALS: *Ayer Directory of Publications*

BOOKS: *Subject Guide to Books in Print*

The following lists of periodicals are by no means all-inclusive. Only items which I have personally found most helpful have been included. In the case of periodicals, write to each of the publishers for a sample copy and subscription information. For books, send for a copy "on approval." The publisher will send you a statement. If you do not wish to keep the book, simply return it for a full cancellation of charges.

PERIODICALS

Administrative Management
51 Madison Avenue, New York, New York 10010

Journal of Business Communication
317b David Kinley Hall, University of Illinois, Urbana, Illinois 61801

Journal of Technical Writing and Communication
Box A-144, Wantagh, New York 11793

Management Review
135 West 50th Street, New York, New York 10020

Nation's Business
1615 H Street, N.W., Washington, D.C. 20006

Direct Marketing
224 Seventh Street, Garden City, New York 11530

Supervisory Management
135 West 50th Street, New York, New York 10020

The Office
P.O. Box 1231, 1200 Summer Street, Stamford, Connecticut 06904

The Writer
8 Arlington Street, Boston, Massachusetts 02116

Writer's Digest
22 East 12th Street, Cincinnati, Ohio 45210

B. SKILL-BUILDING WRITING EXERCISES

Note: Answers to these exercises may be obtained by writing to the publisher. Ask for free "Exercise Answer Key" for *Techniques of Writing Business Letters, Memos, and Reports.*

Exercise 1. Strong Words

Directions: Write words which are stronger than the words listed.

1. ran after
2. seasonal ups and downs
3. bright
4. suddenly rises/goes up
5. moves forward

Exercise 2. Familiar Words

Directions: Write short simple words for each of these words or phrases.

1. inaugurate
2. terminate
3. utilize
4. anticipate
5. assistance
6. endeavor
7. ascertain
8. procure
9. consummate
10. advise
11. alteration
12. forwarded
13. fabricate
14. nevertheless
15. substantial portion
16. fundamental
17. afford an opportunity
18. approximately
19. accomplished
20. accumulate
21. additionally
22. commence
23. compensate
24. demonstrates

25. encounter
26. expedite
27. facilitate
28. initiate
29. indicates
30. maintained
31. objectives
32. obligation

33. participate
34. remittance
35. remuneration
36. subsequent
37. sufficient
38. transmit
39. unavailability
40. voluminous

Exercise 3. Short Words

Directions: Revise these sentences using simple words.

1. The antiquated calculator is ineffectual for solving sophisticated problems.

2. It is imperative that the pay increments be terminated before an inordinate deficit is accumulated.

3. There was unanimity among the executives that Ms. Jackson's idiosyncrasies were cause for a mandatory meeting with the company's personnel director.

4. The impending liquidation of the company's assets was the cause for jubilation among the company's competitors.

5. The expectations of the president for a stock dividend were accentuated because of the preponderance of evidence the company was in good financial condition.

Exercise 4. Concrete Words

Directions: Write a concrete phrase for each of the abstract phrases.

1. sometime this spring

2. a substantial saving

3. a large number attended

4. increased efficiency

5. expanded the work area

Exercise 5. Active Words

Directions: Write each sentence in the active rather than the passive form.

1. The raw data is submitted to the data processing division by the salesmen each Friday.

2. High profits are the responsibility of management.

3. The policies announced in the directive were implemented by the staff.

4. Our typewriters are serviced by the Santee Company.

5. The employees were represented by John Hogan.

Exercise 6. Camouflaged Verbs

Directions: Write each sentence so that the verb is no longer camouflaged.

1.   Adaptation to the new rules was performed easily by the employees.

2.   The assessor will make a determination of the tax due.

3.   Verification of the identity of the employees must be made daily.

4.   The Board of Directors made a recommendation that Mr. Ronson be assigned to a new division.

5.   The auditing procedure on the books was performed by the vice president.

Exercise 7-A. Unnecessary Words

Directions: Select the word(s) which are unnecessary.

1. consensus of opinion
2. exact replica
3. new innovations
4. most unique
5. true facts
6. surrounded on all sides
7. the month of May
8. visible to the eye
9. maximum possible
10. eight in number
11. important essential
12. red in color
13. the state of California

14. my personal opinion
15. entirely complete
16. just recently
17. refer back
18. whether or not
19. continue on
20. past experience
21. long period of time
22. at a distance of 100 feet
23. at a price of $50
24. remember the fact that
25. until such time as
26. I would like to recommend
27. during the course of the
28. he is engaged in reporting on
29. the color of the book is blue
30. the main problem is a matter of scheduling
31. throughout the entire week
32. came at a time when
33. still remains
34. repeat again
35. strict accuracy

Exercise 7-B. Unnecessary Words

Directions: Delete the unnecessary words in these sentences.

1. We are of the conviction that writing is important.
2. In all probability, we're likely to have a price increase.
3. The price increase exceeded the amount of five cents.
4. We are engaged in the process of building this store.
5. Our goals include making a determination about that in the near future.

Exercise 8. Replaceable Phrases

Directions: Rephrase in fewer words.

1. in order so that
2. in the near future
3. in the event that
4. for the purpose of
5. with regard to
6. I am of the opinion that
7. please do not hesitate to let me know
8. I wish to take this occasion to express my thanks
9. the early part of next week
10. your check in the amount of
11. it is quite probable that
12. it may be that
13. at an early date
14. in very few cases
15. with reference to
16. a large number of
17. at the present time
18. there is no doubt that
19. most of the time
20. in the same way

Exercise 9. Infinitive Substitutes

Directions: Use the infinitive as a substitute for these overly-long phrases.

1. In order to live I require money.
2. They did not find sufficient evidence for believing in the future.
3. To bring about the destruction of a dream is tragic.

Exercise 10. Obsolete Phrases

Directions: Write up-to-date versions of these phrases. Write "omit" if you believe there is no appropriate substitute.

1. as per your instruction
2. at an early date
3. attached herewith
4. hold in abeyance
5. in lieu of
6. in reply I wish to state
7. in response to same
8. kindly note same
9. pleased be advised that
10. pursuant to our agreement
11. refer back to
12. take the liberty of
13. thanking you in advance
14. this will acknowledge
15. we wish to advise that
16. yours of the 11th
17. we deem it advisable
18. allow me to express
19. at all times
20. according to our records

Exercise 11. Short Sentences

Directions: Revise these sentences to make them shorter.

1. Next time you write something, check your average sentence length in a 100-word passage and if your sentences average more than 16-20 words, see if you can break up some sentences at the joints.

2. Don't do what the village blacksmith did when he instructed his apprentice as follows: "When I take the shoe out of the fire, I'll lay it on the anvil; and when I nod my head, you hit it with the hammer." The apprentice did just as he was told and now he's the village blacksmith.

3. Unfortunately, there is no button-pressing gadget that will produce excellent writing, but using a yardstick like the Fog Index gives us some guideposts to follow for making writing easier to read because its two factors remind us to use short sentences and simple words.

Exercise 12. Pompous Sentences

Directions: Write these sentences so that they're no longer pompous.

1. During the period of time during which certain acute emergencies arose so that a crisis situation could be said to obtain, individuals rose to the occasion with singular examples of exemplary behavior toward co-workers of close proximity.

2.   Although she functions within the realm of executive-management-level operations, her mental inclination leans toward home and hearth.

3.   He was enabled to obtain a fine position in a custodial engineering capacity at hours which accorded well with his other heavy obligations to family and school.

Exercise 13. Overloaded Sentences

Directions: Condense these sentences to as few words as possible.

1.   When all is said and done at the conclusion of this experiment, I would like to summarize the final wind-up.

2.   After a trial period of three weeks during which time she worked for a total of 15 full working days, we found her work was sufficiently satisfactory so that we offered her full-time work.

3.   I find this is an unexciting, non-stimulating situation.

Exercise 14. Undue Enthusiasm

Directions: Remove the unnecessary intensifiers from these sentences.

1.   Tremendously high pay increases were given to the extraordinarily skilled and extremely conscientious employees.

2. The union demands were highly inflationary, extremely demanding, and exceptionally bold.

Exercise 15. Crowded-Together Sentences

Directions: Make two sentences from each sentence by replacing "and" with a period.

1. Know the flexibility of the written word and its power to convey an idea and know how to make your words behave so your readers will understand.

2. Words mean different things to different people and a word like "block" may mean city block, butcher block, engine block, auction block, block of votes, or several other things.

3. Mineral classifications will be made by areas and these areas will show resources that are available now and it will also show those that will probably become available at sometime in the future.

Exercise 16. Hedging Sentences

Directions: Write these sentences so there's no longer any hedging.

1.   It would appear that someone apparently entered illegally.

2.   I don't really pretend to know anything about art, but it seems to me that particular painting may possibly be one of the most appealing I've seen so far.

3.   It may be possible that sometime in the near future the situation is likely to improve.

Exercise 17. Pronoun Starters

Directions: Write these sentences without a pronoun as the first word of the sentence.

1.   There are several examples here to show that Egbert can't hold a position very long.

2.   It would be greatly appreciated if each and every employee would make a generous contribution to Mildred Splook's retirement party.

3.   It has been learned in Washington today from generally reliable sources that an announcement of great importance will be made shortly by the White House.

Exercise 18. Parallelism

Directions: Present the ideas in these sentences in parallel form.

1. Mr. Hill is expected to lecture three days a week, to counsel two days a week, and must write for publication in his spare time.

2. The office workers were hired to receive callers, to operate the duplicating equipment, and a variety of miscellaneous duties were handled by them.

3. All of the employees were given instruction in writing letters, in using the photocopying machine, and how to keep all of our various accounts in alphabetical order.

Exercise 19. Awkward Pointers

Directions: Revise these sentences so that the awkward pointers can be deleted.

1. The vice president in charge of sales and the production manager are responsible for the key to 34A and 35A respectively.

2. The keys to 34A and 35A are in executive hands with the former belonging to the vice president in charge of sales and the latter belonging to the production manager.

3. The keys to 34A and 35A have been distributed to a vice president and production manager with the aforementioned keys being gold embossed.

Exercise 20. Misassembled Sentences

Directions: Remove the "dangling modifiers" from these sentences.

1. Running down the railroad tracks in a cloud of smoke, we enjoyed a good breakfast in the diner.

2. Lying on the tiny shelf, big Ruby saw the sea shell.

Exercise 21. Tone

Directions: Substitute mild, inoffensive phrases for these phrases.

1. you claim that
2. it is not our policy to
3. you neglected to
4. it is our definite policy
5. in which you assert
6. we are sorry you are dissatisfied
7. you failed to enclose
8. we request that you send us
9. if we are at fault
10. apparently you overlooked our terms
11. we hereby deny your claim
12. we have been very patient
13. we are at a loss to understand
14. you forgot
15. we will be forced to

Exercise 22. "You" Viewpoint

Directions: Write these sentences so they have the "you" viewpoint.

1. We request that you use the order form supplied in the back of our catalog.

2. We insist that you always bring your credit card to the store at all times so that our sales staff does not have to waste their valuable time.

3. We want to get rid of all our typewriters, last year's models, so that we can make room in our warehouse for new models. So, we are offering a 25% discount on all sales this week.

Exercise 23. Positive vs. Negative Viewpoints

1. Unfortunately, your order cannot be sent until next week.

2. To avoid the loss of your credit rating, please remit within 10 days.

3. We don't make refunds on returned merchandise that is soiled.

Exercise 24. Confidence and Conviction

Directions: Rewrite these sentences to show your confidence and conviction.

1. It is our sincere hope that we will hear from you again soon.

2. We feel that you will enjoy owning the Odd-Ark Toy Chest.

3. Perhaps you'll like it well enough to recommend it to your little friends.

4. If possible, please reply by next week.

5. We trust you'll take care of this matter at your earliest convenience.

Exercise 25. Euphemisms

Directions: Put "a nice face" on these words by substituting mild words.

1. unchanging
2. strike (labor)
3. stubborn
4. wrong
5. stupid
6. incompetent
7. small gift
8. loudmouth
9. retail store losses
    (due to theft)
10. poverty

C. CHECKLIST OF
WORDY AND TRITE EXPRESSIONS

Good business writers have condemned many words and phrases as trite, obsolete, and stereotyped. Such words and phrases destroy the modern, efficient business image you are trying to build in your letters.

Here is a list of the worst offenders. The worn out phrases and doublets are on the left, with improved versions on the right.

WORDY/TRITE	IMPROVED
1. a large number of	1. many
2. above numbered policy	2. your policy; this policy
3. absolutely complete	3. complete
4. according to our records	4. we find
5. acknowledging your; answering your	5. (avoid using at the beginning of a letter)
6. advise	6. say; tell
7. agreeable and satisfactory	7. (use just one of the words; not both)
8. allow me to express	8. (just say whatever you wish to say)
9. along the lines of	9. like
10. along this line	10. (omit)
11. and oblige	11. (omit)
12. anxious and eager	12. (use just one of the words; not both)
13. anywheres	13. (no such word as "anywheres," or "somewheres," and "nowheres")
14. are of the opinion that	14. believe
15. as a matter of fact	15. (omit)
16. as in the above	16. (be specific)
17. as per	17. acknowledge

18. as per our letter	18. (do not mix Latin and English)
19. as per your suggestion	19. as you suggested
20. as stated above	20. as we have said.
21. as yet	21. still
22. assuring you of	22. (avoid using)
23. at a later date	23. later
24. at a loss to explain	24. (omit)
25. at all times	25. always
26. at an early date	26. at once (or be more specific)
27. at hand	27. (omit)
28. at the present time	28. now; at present
29. at which time	
30. at your convenience; at an early date	30. immediately (or tell exact date)
31. attached find; attached hereto	31. attached; attached are
32. attached herewith is	32. here is
33. awaiting your	33. (better to say, "May we have your answer at once?")
34. beg to remain	34. (omit)
35. beg to state; beg to advise; beg to acknowledge	35. we are pleased
36. by return mail	36. (be more specific; use "immediately," "at once," or a definite date)
37. claim	37. asserted
38. consensus of opinion	38. (consensus cannot be anything but opinion; say just consensus)

39. contents carefully noted	39. followed in every detail
40. costs the sum of	40. costs
41. courteous and polite	41. (use just one of the words; not both)
42. despite the fact that	42. though, although
43. due to the fact that	43. since, because
44. duly	44. (omit)
45. during the time that	45. while
46. during the time that we were in	46. while we were in
47. during the year of 1970	47. during 1970
48. during this period of time	48. meanwhile; or during this time
49. during which time	49. while
50. each and every one of us	50. each of us; every one of us, all of us
51. enclosed herewith	51. enclosed is
52. enclosed please find	52. we are enclosing
53. endeavor	53. try
54. esteemed	54. (omit; too flowery and effusive)
55. exactly identical	55. identical
56. favor	56. letter, order, or check
57. feel free to	57. please
58. first and foremost	58. (use just one of the words; not both)
59. first of all	59. first
60. for the month of June	60. for June
61. for the period of a year	61. for a year
62. for the purpose of	62. to, for
63. for the purpose of studying	63. to study
64. for the reason that	64. since, because
65. for this reason	65. therefore

66. full and complete	66. (use just one of the words; not both)
67. fully cognizant of	67. aware
68. furnish us with	68. send us
69. give consideration to	69. consider
70. hand you	70. send you; enclose
71. handing you	71. (omit)
72. has come to hand	72. (omit)
73. have before me	73. (omit)
74. hereto	74. (omit)
75. hold in abeyance	75. postpone
76. hope and trust	76. hope
77. hope to receive; hear	77. (avoid using in closing a letter)
78. I have your recent letter at hand	78. I have received; thank you for
79. if and when	79. (use just one of the words; not both)
80. if our records are correct	80. (avoid talking about "our records")
81. in a position to	81. able to
82. in a satisfactory manner	82. satisfactorily
83. in accordance with your request	83. as you requested
84. in addition to the above	84. also
85. in due course; in due time	85. today; tomorrow (or a specific time or date)
86. in lieu of	86. instead
87. in order that	87. so
88. in order to	88. to
89. in re	89. (avoid; state the subject directly)
90. in regard to	90. regarding; about

91. In reply wish to say; in reply would state — 91. (omit)
92. in response to; in reply to — 92. (omit)
93. in response to your favor — 93. (omit)
94. in response to same — 94. in response to it; in response to your recent inquiry
95. in spite of the fact that — 95. because; although
96. in the amount of — 96. for
97. in the city of ——— — 97. in ———
98. in the event that — 98. if; in case
99. in the nature of — 99. like
100. in the near future — 100. soon
101. in the neighborhood of — 101. about
102. in the normal course of our procedure — 102. normally
103. in the very near future — 103. soon
104. in this connection — 104. (omit)
105. in this day and age — 105. today
106. in view of the fact that — 106. since; because
107. in which you assert — 107. you tell us
108. inadvertently — 108. unintentionally
109. inasmuch — 109. since
110. indemnify — 110. protect
111. information which we have in our files — 111. our information
112. inquired as to — 112. asked
113. insist and demand — 113. (use just one of the words; not both)
114. inst.; instant — 114. (use specific date)
115. is not in a position to — 115. cannot
116. it is recognition of this fact that — 116. therefore
117. it is our definite policy — 117. it is our usual practice

118. it is our policy not to	118. we rarely
119. it would be advisable to you	119. I suggest that you
120. kind favor	120. (omit)
121. kind favor; kind order	121. (omit)
122. kindly advise	122. please let us know
123. kindly note same	123. may I call your attention
124. know-how	124. technical knowledge, experience
125. let us hear from you	125. please write us
126. line	126. merchandise; line of goods
127. make an adjustment in	127. adjust
128. may rest assured	128. may be sure
129. most of the time	129. usually
130. must be returned to this office	130. please return
131. my personal opinion	131. my opinion; it cannot be anything but personal
132. not in a position	132. unable
133. of the above date	133. (always give the exact date)
134. of the order of magnitude of	134. about
135. on the grounds that	135. because
136. on the occasion of	136. when, on
137. order has gone forward	137. (tell how and when shipped)
138. our Miss (Mr. or Mrs.)————	138. our representative, Miss————
139. owing to the fact that	139. because
140. party	140. (do not refer to a person as a ''party'')
141. pending receipt of	141. until

142. per diem	142. daily rate
143. permit me to	143. (omit)
144. permit me to say that	144. (permission is not necessary; simply say what you want to say)
145. permit us to state	145. (omit)
146. please be advised that	146. today we have
147. please do not hesitate to write	147. please write
148. please forward a check to cover	148. mail a check for (be specific)
149. please give this matter more attention	149. (be more specific)
150. prior to	150. before
151. proximo	151. (a Latin word meaning "on the next" better to give the exact time of the month)
152. pursuant to our agreement	152. as we agreed
153. pursuant to your request; referring to your letter; in reference to your request	153. (omit)
154. recent date	154. (be specific; use exact date)
155. refer back to	155. refer to
156. regretting that we cannot	156. (omit; do not emphasize "regret")
157. remember the fact that	157. remember
158. reply	158. response; answer
159. replying to	159. (omit)
160. report to the effect that	160. report that

161. right and proper	161. (use just one of the words; not both)
162. said	162. the; this
163. same	163. it; that; them
164. seldom ever; rarely ever	164. seldom; rarely
165. shipment of your order was made	165. shipment was made; your order was shipped
166. sincere and earnest	166. (use just one of the words; not both)
167. sometime in the early part of the coming month	167. early next month
168. state	168. say; tell
169. subsequent to	169. after
170. take pleasure	170. are pleased; happy; glad
171. take this opportunity	171. (omit)
172. taking the liberty of	172. (omit)
173. thanking you in advance	173. (omit)
174. the above named	174. (use the person's name)
175. the reason is due to	175. because
176. the said application	176. application
177. the undersigned	177. I; me
178. the writer	178. I; we
179. there are many people who think that	179. many people think
180. this is to inform you	180. (omit)
181. this matter has been referred to the undersigned	181. this matter has been referred to me
182. this will acknowledge	182. thank you for
183. thought and consideration	183. (use just one of the words; not both)

184. true facts	184. (since facts are true, omit the adjective)
185. trusting you will; trusting this is	185. (omit; shows doubt)
186. ultimo	186. (a Latin word meaning ''the preceding month''; not used in business correspondence)
187. under date of	187. on
188. under separate cover	188. in another envelope; by parcel post, etc.
189. unique as in ''the most unique,'' ''very unique''	189. (unique cannot be qualified; it means one of a kind, without equal)
190. until such time	190. when
191. until such time as	191. until
192. up to this writing	192. (avoid; should state what has taken place)
193. we are at a loss to understand	193. we do not understand
194. we are in receipt of	194. (sounds foo pompous; just write we have received)
195. we are not in a position to	195. we cannot
196. we are of the opinion that	196. we believe
197. we are sorry you are dissatisfied	197. your frank comments are appreciated
198. we cannot proceed to	198. we can (be positive)

199. we hereby deny your claim	199. we cannot honor your claim
200. we hope; we trust	200. (avoid; shows doubt)
201. we remain	201. (omit)
202. we should like benefit of	202. we need
203. we take this opportunity	203. (omit)
204. we will be forced to	204. you will compel us to
205. we wish to advise that	205. (omit)
206. will appreciate; will be glad; will be pleased	206. shall, will
207. will you advise me	207. will you let me know
208. will you be kind enough to	208. please
209. wish to; would like to	209. (omit; be more direct)
210. with a view to	210. to
211. with the result that	211. so that
212. with reference to; with regard to; with respect to	212. about
213. within the course of the next two days	213. within two days
214. without further delay	214. now, immediately
215. without making any noise	215. noiselessly
216. you failed to enclosed	216. you did not enclose
217. you neglected to send	217. you did not send
218. you owe a total of $500	218. you owe $500
219. your check in the amount of $500	219. your check for $500
220. your letter under date of	220. your letter of
221. yours of the 12th	221. (be specific: "Your letter of June 12.")